My Pet Zoo

Story by Janie Spaht Gill, Ph.D.
Illustrations by Bob Reese

DOMINIE PRESS

Pearson Learning Group

"I need a pet.

Which one should I get?"

3

"I'll sweep," said the sheep.

"I'll rake," said the snake.

7

"I'll box," said the fox.

"I'll laugh," said the giraffe.

"I'll chew," said the kangaroo.

13

"I'll kneel," said the seal.

"I'll cheer," said the deer.

"Oh, dear, what shall I do?"

"I'll take them all

and start a zoo."

Curriculum Extension Activities

- Retell the story using drama. The children could draw the animal faces on construction paper, cut them out, and then staple them to a strip of tag board. The children could bring actual props from home to depict things that the animals used in the book, or they could draw them on sheets of construction paper.

- Make a class mural of a zoo. Paint or draw the cages, trees, water, caves, etc. The children can then draw the animals in the appropriate habitats.

- Ask the children to draw and cut out their favorite animal in the story. Under each drawing, have them write the name of the animal. Arrange the animals on a chart, first from lightest to heaviest, and then in alphabetical order.

- If possible, take the children on a field trip to a zoo. If a visit to a zoo is out of the question, show them a video featuring zoo animals, or have someone involved with animal care come and talk to the class.

About the Author

Dr. Janie Spaht Gill brings twenty-five years of teaching experience to her books for young children. During her career thus far, she has taught at every grade level, from kindergarten through college. Gill has a Ph.D. in reading education, with a minor in creative writing. She is currently residing in Lafayette, Louisiana with her husband, Richard. Her fresh, humorous topics are inspired by the things her students say in the classroom. Gill was voted the 1999-2000 Louisiana Elementary Teacher of the Year for her outstanding work in primary education.

Softcover Edition ISBN 0-7685-2149-1
Library Bound Edition ISBN 0-7685-2457-1

Printed in Singapore
  5 6 7 8 9 10   10 09 08 07

Dominie
Press

Pearson Learning Group

1-800-321-3106
www.pearsonlearning.com